FAR MORE THAN A BOOK

Destinations in Heavenly Places

Haley Keen

ISBN 979-8-89309-442-8 (Paperback)
ISBN 979-8-89309-443-5 (Digital)

Copyright © 2024 Haley Keen
All rights reserved
First Edition

All rights reserved. No part of this publication may be reproduced, distributed, or transmitted in any form or by any means, including photocopying, recording, or other electronic or mechanical methods without the prior written permission of the publisher. For permission requests, solicit the publisher via the address below.

Covenant Books
11661 Hwy 707
Murrells Inlet, SC 29576
www.covenantbooks.com

CONTENTS

Introduction v

Chapter 1: My New Beginning 1
Chapter 2: Picked by Jesus 4
Chapter 3: Ever-changing Beauty 7
Chapter 4: Adorned Birthright 9
Chapter 5: The Original Potter 12
Chapter 6: My Finisher, Beginner, and Transitioner 15
Chapter 7: Overcoming in the Misty Manna 18
Chapter 8: Our Ordained Supper 22
Chapter 9: The Journey Has Just Begun 25

Invitations for Jesus and the Holy Spirit 27
Key Scriptures That Bring This Book Life 29
Intriguing Symbolisms 35

INTRODUCTION

I am so excited for you to read *Far More Than a Book: Destinations in Heavenly Places*! This book is about how extraordinarily the Holy Trinity loves us and wants to encounter us in amazing ways. It showcases how the gifts God gives us are so very important and how He will encounter us through them. He can use your gifts to encounter you in the unique ways He has designed. We get to see a way He does this through the writing of this book. This book holds my personal experiences with the Holy Spirit, through visions and interpretation. I believe that sharing these facts and experiences will make it even more impactful for others. I hope that you experience new wonders of God through inspiration from this book.

CHAPTER 1

My New Beginning

One Wednesday evening, after I had come home from church, I started to not feel very well. I cleaned my face and began to prepare myself for the night. I began to feel frustrated and had a headache. So I stood firm in the Lord, whom I trust as my God, and in His promises, and I began to speak some of His Words over my life. I felt horrible but was persistent in my faith, and what I knew I needed to do to feel better. Suddenly, I felt extremely prompted to write in my journal, which I write in often.

Out of the spirit of obedience and breakthrough, I sat down and put my pen to paper. While I did this, I was reminded of something the Holy Spirit had previously shown and shared with me: that there is "power in the pen." I saw a vision of a written statement sentence in a big book that was in heaven. I also saw a hand that was writing a statement sentence on earth. Then an angel was writing that same statement sentence that the hand was writing, under the original statement sentence that was written in the big book in heaven. This angel was very small compared to the size of the book. After this, I realized that when we, as people, write, say, do, put action to, or embody any of the characteristics of God in the form of action, something amazing happens. If what we are doing aligns with what is written about our purposes in life, we fulfill a sentence!

In this vision, somebody was fulfilling the purpose of a sentence while writing and an angel was assisting in making this happen. I was strongly reminded in my spirit that there is "power in the pen." My pen was just sitting on my journal, waiting for me to fulfill sentences! I couldn't help but want to be obedient. The Holy Spirit then said to me that if I trust Him, He will guide me and do something so extraordinary that I had never experienced before. So I began to move my pen, and that's when obedience and new revelation opened access for God to bring His hand down and sweep me into what would be the former unknown.

I saw the hand of the Lord pick me up and bring me into a land of unknown wonders. I could barely move my body, but my spirit was doing jumping jacks! I was introduced to a land that seemed like another world. This place was thriving, and the people were filled with zeal and commitment. I watched what I could see was happening while sitting at the very top of a mountain. The altitude was rich, but not foggy. It was one of the clearest experiences I had ever encountered at that time. The clouds were neither too high above me nor too low. I was sitting on the top of this mountain, filled with the presence of God! My body remained still because it knew it was on holy ground. It felt as if my body knew before my mind could comprehend where I was. Thick golden glory, in the form of a mist, was floating around me in a half-circle, although it left open a clear window of entrance to witness what was being displayed for me to see below. There were also golden clouds carrying glory, floating around me. I was so caught up in the presence of the Lord!

I played with these clouds, filled, radiating, and exuding God's glory with my hands. They rose upward as I touched them, and what looked like small shapes of fireworks, which were of glory essence, appeared and went off. My head, along with my whole body, felt light and carefree as I started to relax and have fun. The joy that I had in this particular moment was precious! I felt safe watching and playing with these glory clouds.

At that time, I had forgotten about what was happening below. I no longer saw the clear window because I was caught up in something so tangibly captivating! When I noticed this, I saw what looked like walls of glory that were more solid than the mist and essence.

They appeared and slowly moved away from each other, exposing great white light that shined in a piercing manner.

I could not see what the Lord had prepared for me to see behind the light for a short while because the light was so bright and broadly concentrated toward my eyes and center of focus. It felt as if my brain was releasing mixed signals and was on several kinds of alert. I was fearful, excited, pleased, and full of questions all at the same time! This was a moment that would jolt me into answered prayers, heart's desires, and promises from the Lord, spoken to my heart years before.

CHAPTER 2

Picked by Jesus

When the light took a break from further instilling the fear of the Lord in me, its brightness calmed down to a comfortable shade, and I saw a place that I thought might be where high-ranked officials of heaven reside. They were intent on the Lord and seemed busy with what they were doing. There was no doubt, questions, or any sign of uncertainty concerning them. The obedience they have for God is tangibly magnificent! Everything in this place had its purpose and place.

Everything has a sound and creates an effect with its presence. Most importantly, everything carries and exudes the presence of God. While observing this, I felt the presence of the Lord's hand, and every trace of tension that I had melted away. As I noticed this, I felt what I immediately knew was God's breath or the Holy Spirit. It was a sweet sensation, but not completely clear, although it was not supposed to be clear to me immediately.

What I then realized was that the wind that came from God was His breath that the Holy Spirit granted me access to experience at that moment. I could feel life in it, even as it passed me. It lingered on and with me, as to claim and clothe me with its revelation, love, freedom, and peace. I had never felt something so refreshing since the moment I was created with His breath. I do not currently remember it, but I am convinced that it was even more refreshing in many ways. When this thought and realization began to come to an end, a whirlwind of God's breath-filled wind came after me in a tender way. It entered my nose, filling my chest with the coolest, freshest feeling of water I had ever felt. I was hungry for more of this water, even as it was filling me. I was not thirsty, but hungry for more of God and for Him to show more of His wonders in and through my body. I wanted Him to show and fill my body with another wonder, but with one of His strengths at that moment. I then started to feel my muscles pump with energy and fortitude. My veins felt the presence of Jesus. My mind was overcoming every sorrow of a former weak body.

Shortly after that, something I had pondered could happen in my past happened. Everything I had dealt with and everything I had overcome was displayed in front of me in the presence of God. I was exposed. Father God decided He wanted to make it definitively clear how He knows everything about me and does not miss a thing. He did this in front of my eyes and in all the places I would encounter. I was not overcome with sorrow, embarrassment, or shame. I was shocked and convicted by His love. I was overwhelmingly thankful to see and be in a place that I had never been before, although I had eagerly longed to. I was watching pieces of my God's grandeur at work in my life. I was so moved in my spirit I could not cry tears.

What was happening in my spirit felt like a ginormous herd of cattle or elephants running as fast as they could to get a drink of water—a drink of water from somewhere they had never been before and from a place that holds the best, most rejuvenating, and safest waters. I could not help but leap toward what I knew was God right in front of me, although I could not clearly see Him.

My mind was so blown that my spirit had to do the thinking and deciding. My heart poured out repentance and immense joy at the same time. That is when Jesus's hand caught me! He looked at me with the most loving smile I had ever seen. I felt such completeness, and I knew that this was just the beginning. I could feel my whole life changing in Jesus's hand. I could feel everything about me being fully healed and changing for advancement. I began to realize that I was an honored guest in heaven, who had been expected and anticipated! I was here for more than revelation and a wonderful experience.

This was a complete life-changing opportunity. This had been prepared for me and was also preparing me for the near and distant future. The honor that I felt was so intense. I felt so loved and appreciated! Honor for God, and His display of honor for those who are ready for it, was extremely grand, massive, and everywhere around me. I noticed Jesus was carrying me somewhere. This gave me great delight! My heart was trying to calm down from all the incredible emotions and traits of God it was feeling, but it could not. Eventually, oil started to pour out of me, from my heart. Rich, fragrant oil flowed from my being. It was doing this because my heart could not contain what was happening to it as it was being anointed and being prepared to enter the most holy place I have ever encountered. When we approached this place that goes further into heaven, I saw angels in uneven kinds of lines on two different sides, leading to an entrance with a humongous, solid, gold, double-wide door. The door was shut and radiating glory.

When Jesus and I got close enough, He went up to the door and put one of His shining hands on it! After He did this, He said, "It is time to open for her. She is ready!" As I continued to sit in His hand, I started to feel like it was the most normal yet extraordinary thing to happen. I felt the innocence, faith, and full trust of a child wash over me in a new way. I could not help but be obedient once again, and I liked it that way. It never felt so natural to be invited and called upon by God. It also never felt so natural to be interceded for by Jesus. When He told the door to open and that I was ready, I got to witness a way He intercedes for me. This experience was stunningly amazing yet so natural within me and all my senses! Jesus has a great smile that beams with authority. He knew what I was feeling and thinking! I could feel His joy as He was holding and carrying me to Father God!

The joy of Jesus is so supernatural and real. It is like no other, yet it intermingles with God and the Holy Spirit, while also spending time with the children of God. I learned that we can continually host the joy of Jesus, as well as the Holy Trinity, inside ourselves! We can also host and welcome His joy everywhere we go, and in everything we set our feet, hands, authorities, and responsibilities to. We can do this with the authority and love of His name and relationship with His Holy Trinity. What a closer friend and understanding I would have in Jesus from that point on!

CHAPTER 3

EVER-CHANGING BEAUTY

I had never felt love the way I was experiencing it at that moment; not even the love of the Lord that I had known prior to what I am sharing now. God is always the same, but what I had previously known was coming into realignment and a new order. It was increasingly substantial in magnitude! When Jesus released His hand from the door, it started to shake and quake in an exciting kind of way. This signaled to me to prepare myself! My spirit was still rapidly stirring, although I had a new peace and discovery of normalcy in God's presence. My eyes were attentive and wide open.

As the humongous double-wide doors opened, I could feel that there were eyes looking upon me. The opening of these doors had a great bright light, like the first light when the glory walls opened. However, this light was golden, deeper, and surprisingly had a form of gentleness. This gentleness calmed me. As the gentleness was doing this, I realized that it is an attitude of Father God's heart. I knew no matter what God wanted to do with me when I fully entered, that I would be taken good care of and handled with tenderness. Then like a porcelain doll that is elegant and poised and holds a beauty that I could not see grow or flourish, I entered willingly while still being in Jesus's hand.

I was watching as I was being brought through what looked like courtrooms of heaven. The moving eyes of heavenly beings were watching the beauty I had once known transform. All of a sudden, parts of me that I had never felt before started to come to life and move fluently! I felt a way I did not know I could feel. I became something I did not even know about! I entered unknown parts of myself and how I was made! God knew, Jesus knew, the Holy Spirit knew, the angels, and heaven knew these new parts of me that I was just now experiencing. So did my future, from the moment I chose to fully submit to God, and they all still do.

    I felt like an instrument created long ago that was hidden from the world, hidden until someone had the desire and longing to discover and uncover it. I felt truly introduced for the first time, with more "bells and whistles" than I could count. I felt distinct kinds of beauty with different avenues dwelling in me and pouring out of me that were not solely my own! I felt the transformation of healing, and my identity drastically extending. I had been praying and longing for this to happen, and it happened in an instant. The porcelain doll that I was used to feeling like came to a blunt and amazing end. The journey that brought me to this never left me the same.

CHAPTER 4

Adorned Birthright

I climbed down from Jesus's hand as He lowered me down to the holy ground, while I was still feeling the beginning effects of transformation. I started dancing uninterrupted as soon as my feet hit the ground! My moments were filled with pure joy, energy fueled by the Spirit of God, breakthroughs, answered prayers, and the beauty of promise! I danced and danced, as melodies came out of my mouth and exuded out of my movements.

There was a grace that I do not know how to explain, clothing me and beauty accenting me as symbolizing accessories. I could feel and see that there was a flower in my hair. It was big, healthy, and a beautiful red that drew the eye. I also felt a dress cascading over me, extending into a short, ruffled, circular train with an opening at the front. It was elegant with a white sash tied around its purple frame. It had puffed golden, purple, and white sleeves. The white color resembled an ivory and cream color with elegant, precise crinkles. The gold swirled into designs and brought a pleasing sight to my eyes, as did the whole dress.

I stopped dancing to examine the dress and was approached by a heavenly being, giving me what looked like a small bowl. This bowl looked like it was sculpted out of a shell. It was brown on the outside and the same color white as my dress on the inside. It held very deep blue waters that made waves in the bowl. The heavenly being gave me this bowl of water for me to drink. As I drank this water, with the first taste, I was standing on waves of very deep blue water, just like the water in the bowl! I was in another heavenly destination.

In the near distance, there was a sunrise happening; however, the sky already had light. There were orange, yellow, red, grapefruit colors, and some dark blue colors slowly rising from a base. Then I saw an essence that I knew had to be my Father God, on a shore in the middle of the waters, just a few steps ahead of me. When I saw this and tried to understand what it meant, He said to me, "You can make the leap." The way he said this was filled with so much peace, confidence, faith in me, and His abilities to see me through it, that it gave me all the motivation and encouragement I needed to have my senses pushing me forth, to jump across the remaining water!

With one leap of instant obedience, faith, and love, I was there on the shore with God. When I noticed that I had landed, the once tan sand turned into a beautiful, vibrant, bright blue. There were seashells in the sand. Some were holding oils, and some held unique types of candy. Just by seeing the candy inside these shells, I could taste the good, rich sweetness that warmed my soul from some of them. From others, I could taste fruity tangs that energized my soul. One had a familiar taste, like rose, but it was creamy. This was completely new to me! There were also some candies with the taste of grapes, limes, cucumbers, oranges, strawberries, dates, bananas, and coconuts. These fruity flavors were so much better than anything I have tasted on Earth. They taste similar enough to recognize, but also very different. They are bursting with so much life! I experienced what felt like a whole new kind of joy regarding candy.

My focus shifted to see a clam with a purple mouth. Its shell had a mix of ivory and cream white, similar to the colors on my dress. It opened its mouth, and when I was done observing its outer appearance, it revealed a giant pink pearl on its green tongue. It was definitely the most unique sea creature I had ever seen at the time. God was still there, while I was observing and experiencing all of this. He was watching me the whole time!

The clam then began to speak and said, "Take what's yours." I had always expected that animals could talk, a sea creature in this case. It was so shocking and cool that I began to laugh in the form of giggling, although I knew what this clam was telling me to do was extremely important.

I took a moment to look at God. It felt so normal. I did not understand it at first. I saw how excited He was for me. I saw how He was anticipating and waiting for me to look at Him and see His excitement that does not go away. He was waiting to see how I was going to pick up the giant pink pearl in the clam's mouth and what would happen after that, and the rest of my life!

This is when I heard God say, "Pick up the pearl. Receive your birthright!" *Wow!* is a good word to describe this. (One of my two birthstones is a pearl.) God is so personal with His people and was displaying this to me in that moment.

CHAPTER 5

THE ORIGINAL POTTER

I went to pick up the giant pearl that kept growing. It was so heavy that God placed His hand beneath mine to help me pick it up and carry it to our next destination. Before we went on to our next destination, He looked into my eyes, while holding the now more than massive pearl with me. All I could see in His eyes was a shape with great light that was not being displayed in its fullness and a deep, bright blue that grew in intensity. I could feel His eyes staring deep within me, with love and the attitude of the original Father that He is. His eyes were so close! They were so close that it looked like I could touch them. This is an experience that I know will grow deeper and deeper throughout my life and is still happening now!

God then spoke to me again, saying, "I have searched your heart thoroughly. Come, and take your place where the heroes roam. Come, be in a place fitted by me for queens that are mature to rule with the Spirit of grace, and where kings echo the commands of My heart. Come, take your seat which is unlike any other. Take refuge on the road I have placed you on, and everywhere it leads. I am your road doused with traits and qualities that welcome you to what the world says is impossible." Those words sunk into my being. My heart started pounding as He brought the pearl we were holding to my chest. This is when He placed the pearl representing my birthright into my heart. Now my heart carries it everywhere I go!

He then transported us to His Potter's Workshop. The Potter's Workshop was the biggest place I had seen thus far in one setting! I could not even see all of it. There were vases, jugs, jars, corks, bottles, sculptures, so much water, fire, swirls of breath in many different colors, and lumps of clay. These were some of the Potter God's works in process, along with His tools. The clay was spotlighted as a main and extremely important part of the learning experience in this destination.

I was in a room where God creates, reforms, and restructures! It is where His fire, water, and breath bring His creative will to life. I was about to witness something much more than incredible. There were lumps of clay with indentations, and structures of clay that looked like they were being sculpted with much care. These structures had great detail and had to do with people! They were alive, but not moving except for when God would place His hands and use His tools on them. I stood watching God look very busy as light shined from and around His figure. When God put His hands on these clay structures, crinkles formed in the clay that was wet from His water. When He put His hands on the lumps of clay with indentations, it was from what I could tell, His power punching the lumps of clay! These pieces of clay were not yet being chiseled and carved into beautiful structures, like the other pieces of clay. They were being transformed from being almost lifeless. With God's enormous power punches, one of the lumps of clay started to slim in an inward motion and grow tall! It was unstructured but moving, by His power.

I received revelation from the Holy Spirit on how these lumps of clay represent people. People who are beginning to trust God and let Him change them. The structures of clay are people who have already been through the process that the lumps of clay "people" are experiencing. They are being chiseled in finer detail. They are becoming mature, with smiling faces, as Father God does His work—the work of the original Potter.

God then motioned for me to follow Him as He started walking down a hallway with lines of clay people structures on each side. It looked like each person's structure was being showcased with an expression of joy on their faces and a kind of spotlight shining on them. There was a space between each one. They were pleasant and hard to stop looking at. We kept walking through this hallway while I looked at these personal structures. They represent humans at their greatest peaks in life with God. I then saw that we were walking on an exceedingly long, narrow, and vibrant, dark blue carpet. This carpet is where the spotlights were shining from, illuminating the people's structures. These lights were shining with a great bluish-white iridescence. This sight made me want to smile. As I continued to follow God down this long narrow hallway, I could see us walking in a dark blue atmosphere.

In the atmosphere was a streak of very bright, luminous blue light flying around with great speed, making infinity signs! It then flew with incredible speed ahead of us, moving as a torch leading the way ahead. God was beaming with radiant enthusiasm and excitement. He laughed and smiled with such beauty and a bounty of the wonders and nature of who He is. I heard Him say with the most enthusiastic, ecstatic, experience-filled voice that I had ever heard, and now know, "Let's go!"

CHAPTER 6

My Finisher, Beginner, and Transitioner

He took my hand and pulled me through an average-sized, white, glowing door, although it was not average at all. The other side of this door was filled with blossoming greenery and flowers! There was a magnificent river with a waterfall. I had never seen waters so blue and white at the same time. The river, flowing down from the waterfall, was teeming with the life of imagination! The river was rapid in speed and incredibly strong. I wanted to know the purpose of this river as I was standing in front of it. God was standing next to me, and He said, "Place your hand on the waves that are gentle on this river." I did so and saw a vision of every creative thought I had that was fueled by God. They were swirling around me in my bedroom in the form of these waters from this river.

I was watching this vision as if I were on the other side of a looking glass and adventure. He told me that He gave me the creativity, fortitude, and access to get to where I am now. Like a river, I flow with what His spirit has told, shown, and previously shared with me. Now I get to become like a waterfall that always pours out His thirst-quenching revival at rapid, increasing speeds. Operating in and sharing His beauty is becoming almost effortless for me in many ways. How I twinkle like the stars' light and draw fascination from people as to what I have and am discovering and learning, have favored access to, and get to do in display and privacy with Him. I then heard a different voice say, "He is the finisher, beginner, and transitioner! Watch your new story unfold."

When this voice stopped speaking, I was standing in a massive field of pure white snow, next to a warm orange burning fire, on top of a stack of wood logs. I did not see anyone there at first. I looked down at my hands which were cold and saw gloves on them that were not there before. They were puffy, blue, and only had a thumb hole, like ski mittens. They were heavy-duty.

As I looked at these gloves, I noticed that my dress had transitioned into a red ski outfit that was fit for activity. It had a zipped-up, long, red jacket and red pants that were of the same material as the gloves. I reached into the pockets of my new jacket to find what looked and felt like a key in one of them. It was heavy and gold with no edges but straight and smooth. Then an angel appeared, looked straight at me, and said, "You have the key. What do you think you should do with it?" Stunned, I answered through action. I quickly threw the key into the fire that was next to me. Right after I did that, the fire started bubbling and turning a passionate pink. The sight of this now pink fire in the middle of the field of pure white snow was beautiful and burned with a bright new clarity!

I stared in awe and wondered at what my action was carrying out. I then heard a voice from the sky saying, "The joy of the Lord is like a sword." A sword then started to quickly appear in the angel's hand. It was of shining blue and white fire that was consistently moving and sparkling. I felt the pull of the Holy Spirit deep within my own spirit, and a huge, great draw toward this sword. The angel moved its hand, which was firmly holding the sword, toward me with much authority. The angel then said, what the clam had said to me earlier, "Take what's yours." So I received the sword from its hand, and the angel immediately started showing me how to use it. What a sight it is to be *trained* by an angel on how to use a sword from God. I felt like I was encountering myself, being further commissioned for something great.

This sword was very warm, with a golden handle that looked like it had carved lines around it, in chiseled perfection. The sword was too heavy to move, but I had a feeling that I was born to hold this sword. This honor, the new responsibility of obtaining and learning how to use and wield this sword, was all a birthright of mine. Another piece of my birthright was then placed in my heart to carry. I started practicing formation with the sword, while the angel was close by watching. My natural instincts came out, knowing how to move this sword of joy and access its power. This power was much more than happiness. This power was intense and had my focus. My hand felt tingly like there was a heat from the Lord over, on, and in it. It was humid but refreshing, and starting to extend its flames into a reddish-pink color. I could feel stinging sweat pouring from my head and body, as if I were losing the weight of baggage, and my muscles were being refined.

While practicing formation with the sword, I could feel that my legs were different. I looked down to see that my legs had become muscular and defined, as my pants were turning into shorts. My legs were smooth with no trace of the discoloration that I had formerly experienced. Then my arms followed along, with my whole body, while my long sleeves were shrinking like my pants were. Refining that comes in training, battle, and authority was taking place. I knew that Potter God had just shifted something in and about my structure of clay.

When I realized this, I heard a hearty, joyful laugh from God, coming through the sky. I looked up to the sky with a serious kind of smile. As I did this, I put the flaming sword of joy on my shoulder. The sword had extended further into a yellow color, complementary to the reddish-pink that surrounded the core of blue and white colors. I could feel that it was time to go to the next place in this planned adventure by God. Holding my sword on my shoulder, as if to symbolize, "I'm packed and ready to go," I wondered what would await me next.

CHAPTER 7

OVERCOMING IN THE MISTY MANNA

My next moment was in a place filled with a very bright, concentrated yellow light, bolder than the sun. I stood in this place, unable to see anything but layers of yellow. It was almost like what I would call a *fuzzy kind* of atmosphere, containing an even thicker mist than the mists I had encountered before. This time, it was foggy or fuzzy. This mist was alive and was some kind of presence. It was so fresh and beautiful. It was a feeling of, "Wow! Look where I'm at now." I was filled with so much amazement about this type of presence that I could not identify. Then unexpectedly, I burst into tears. Tears flowed from my eyes and from a place deep within my core. I had already been so transformed during these encounters. I expected more transformation, but not to feel that much sorrow, especially in the heavenly presence.

Every piece of broken heart that was not hiding from God, but from me, came to my attention. This was a way deeper kind of exposure than what I previously encountered in these experiences. This exposure was more than *seeing* what I was going through before. That was amazing alone, but this experience increased my portion of healing. I then felt a forceful pulling inside of me, telling me, "Search your belief no matter how much you overcome, and how far you go." When I heard this, the tears coming from my eyes literally froze on my cheeks and in my eyes.

The tears in my eyes that froze became like *see-through* ice. Seeing through the ice, I began to watch where my belief had been. I had fully believed that God would transform me, further me, bring me to deeper encounters than I had ever had before, and fulfill His purpose for my life before I experienced any of these encounters. However, my emotions had trouble going "all in." This was the state of my earthly life's process. It soon became abundantly clear to me that I was not just in heaven. I was also with the Holy Spirit but still anchored in my body at the same time.

My emotions were experiencing healing. This process was bringing down healing, grace, forgiveness, and a new anointing of peace to my body and soul. Then my body, soul, and spirit reacted in excitement, while transformation and peace began to release troubles. As a result, all of me became changed, in healing advancement. I stopped crying and looked up from my position, where I had ended up on the ground, crouching. Then with a big quick scoop, I pulled in some of the yellow presence mist. I then breathed in this thick mist of heavenly presence. I still did not know what this presence was, other than it was heavenly.

As I breathed in deeper and deeper, the sorrow I was feeling slowly left in a few *new kinds of* moments. In these moments, I was breathing in and out. When I would breath out, the yellow presence of mist came out of my mouth, blowing in a subtle way. It still held presence and appearance, however. I sat there for a while, breathing in and out, watching the yellow mist come out of my mouth and through my nose, forming circles. Circles floated out to the distance, getting bigger and bigger. That is when my outfit changed again. It changed into a flowing white dress, symbolizing my going through and experiencing a new depth of being an overcomer. I wiped my eyes and smiled.

After this, I felt such a sensation of sleepiness. I had been in some of the most amazing, exciting places, although I had a feeling of exhaustion, but not weariness. I yawned with the countenance of a sleepy child, ready for a nap. Two angels brought a blanket made of stars and clouds and placed it over me. It covered all of me, except my head, face, and hair. They began to sing, "Go to sleep, go to sleep, mighty one. Go to sleep, go to sleep, precious one. Go to sleep, go to sleep, sweet child of God. Go to sleep." They also added my name in some of these lines. I fell asleep to their melody and words while remembering lullabies sung to me as a child. I felt such a beautiful, permanent kind of reprieve and real relief from the past. While my eyes were closed and I was asleep, I felt the shaking of what I knew were bricks. Even in my sleep, I could see they were red and old. They were falling, no crashing, off my life and everything having to do with it. The destination of bricks was one of catastrophe, but my next destination would be one of exuberant freedom!

During the next phase of my journey, the two angels never left me. In fact, other angels joined to form a herd. Each one knew what it was to do, concerning me and for its eternity. I was still asleep as they were flying me. I was then covered with two blankets instead of just one. One was made of stars, a dark blue sky, and parts of the moon! The other one was the same one as before, made of stars and clouds, but this time there was also a sun on it. It was brighter and held notes of gold. The blanket made of pieces of the moon was under me, representing a kind of night. The one made of clouds was on top of me, representing a kind of day.

Though I was asleep, I was still sensing, seeing, and hearing. I started hearing how greatly massive the wings of the angels were, while they were still flying me. "Whoosh, whoosh," their wings were saying. I could see that some had white and brown feathered wings, while others had glittery white wings that went up and down. Even the sleeping I was doing was so godly supernatural. It was like resting in the middle of two dimensions and having access to both. I felt a bounty of beauty as I was sleeping, gaining, and experiencing rest in heaven. It was becoming to me. I fit in perfectly, in every experience!

What a joy it is to be this favored, to be this cared for, thought about, and chosen! What a supernatural normalcy it should be for all people who will choose Jesus and accept experiences with the Holy Trinity. This is a beautiful right to God's people from Him, but it does not always take place in the natural, or solely in the natural. As I was feeling this expression from my heart, I did not want to stop going to different destinations in heavenly places, although I did

FAR MORE THAN A BOOK

want to arrive at a place where I was meant to linger. The lingering that I would soon experience would become the most amazing part of my journey in these places.

CHAPTER 8

Our Ordained Supper

I woke up suddenly to be put down by the angels. I was in an exceptionally large hall that looked like a room that went on and on. It was light gold and champagne colored. This place definitely looked like it required an invitation. At first, I couldn't see anybody in this place. I walked around the room, observing what looked like white sculpted clay designed on the walls. They resembled the ones we have on Earth, in wealthy homes, establishments, and architecture from some of the eras before now. I trailed down the hall, further and further, basking in the light it hosted. I smiled, even laughed, during this stroll in heaven. I felt so at home that I started to sing, "I was waiting for God. I was waiting for His grand surprises to change my life! What a God I get to know!"

I then started whistling with my fingers in my mouth, something I could never do before. I was just about to sing another line when I stopped in my tracks to see the hall I was traveling down had ended. It ended and went straight to the top of a waterfall! By the time I realized this, I already had my feet on water. I quietly gathered myself and sat on the waters I was standing on. I was confident that I would be more than fine. The waters below me were steady and calm. I then closed my eyes so I could hear better. When I did this, the waters I was sitting on picked up a pace that moved my body closer and closer to the edge. They became rapid and rampaging.

That's when my spirit told me to jump. After what was probably a split second of thought, I obeyed the instruction. I remembered

God telling me earlier how "I could make the leap." With that very memory propelling me, with more motivation, I stood up, spread my arms out, and jumped down into the rampaging waterfall!

When I opened my eyes, I was safely standing on the rapid waters. My attention was then directed toward Jesus, drawing me to Himself. He was sitting on a basic-looking wooden chair at a round wooden table. The furniture was floating on these waters! The waters were calm and collected where Jesus was, but where I was, the waters were still rapid and rampaging. Everything about the moment was planned by Father God, as well as every destination that I had encountered.

As I was focused on Jesus and processing my surroundings, He motioned his hand signaling, "Come." The way He did this looked so effortless and so casual, although I knew this was important. I looked down at the busy-looking waters under my feet and then started to move my feet toward Jesus. The rampaging waters calmed as I was walking on them! My attention went fully back on Jesus. As I got closer to the table, I could feel Jesus's eyes peering into me, like Father God did earlier. I felt so seen and recognized! His eyes were so intent on me and still are to this day! Even when I went to sit down on the chair across from Him, He was still staring into my eyes. When I say this, I do not mean at my eyes. I literally mean into my eyes. He was looking into every part of who I am the whole time.

When I was seated, I saw grapes, red pears, what looked like a loaf of chocolate challah bread, and some food I was not familiar with, on the table. The table and chairs looked simple, but the place settings at the table were gold and fancy. This time I noticed how Jesus was dressed. He looked to be wearing a soft, knee-length, brown tunic. Jesus is so representational and understanding. I always knew this, but in the presence of an encounter, it feels like everything changes.

Jesus took the loaf of chocolate challah bread and broke it, without asking me if I wanted any. He placed one half on my plate, and then the other half on His. He looked ready and excited to eat, but before He did, He asked me a question in such normalcy. He said, "How have you liked your time here so far?" He was still looking into me, in His knowing ways, but still expecting me to answer.

I answered Him saying, "I am known here and unconditionally loved. There are no lies here. Everything that is said is of truth and righteousness! In every place that I have been to here, there was a place and purpose for me. Everything here seems to currently know more about me than I do! Nothing here denies You. You are absolute! You are worthy! You are infinite!" In tears, I continued, "I used to think that these kinds of experiences would happen in different ways and at different times. You have plans but also adventures, experiences, encounters, and journeys that seem spontaneous, for Your people. During these destinations in heaven, I have seen things that people say are impossible! I have also seen wonders confirming what Your Holy Spirit has been trying to communicate to me, that I was not fully understanding! I am awake and I am alive! I am not dead during these times of encounters in heavenly destinations. I am so, so alive, bursting with living water and color! I am bombarded by Your goodness and treasures at every turn. I am not shown as simple here. Every part of me is uniquely emphasized! Your chairs and table look simple, but they are not! They hold mysteries and representations. I am learning here. I am welcome here. I have been further changed here! My story weaves into Yours, as Yours does into mine, and will continue to forever! You have shown me, while all of this is extraordinary, it is also meant to be a kind of normalcy. Your grandly infinite love for relationship and covenant has surrounded me in such ways. It engulfs me, with refining revelation of how You favor, love, and know Your people and creation. How You know, favor, and love me! I am honored to sit at Your wooden table. I am so honored that You wanted me to come closer and closer, and still do! I am touched that You listen to me the ways You do, like how You are listening to me right now!"

With a tear-filled smile, I finished what I would say to Him during this encounter. "Getting to talk to You in this setting is so amazingly special to me. Even as You peer into me, You are taking care of me and affirming me with Your gaze! What a beauty You are, and what a great privilege it is to know You! To know You in ways that always substantially increase! Your Holy Trinity is my heart's desire and the fuel to my entire existence."

CHAPTER 9

The Journey Has Just Begun

When I finished speaking, Jesus said to me with a loving smile, "I love you too." The sound of this sentence lasted and echoed during the rest of our time here. After a pause, He continued saying, "Now I want you to go ahead and eat what I put before you on your plate. You are going to need it! Now that you know these things and have seen them in these ways, I am going to need you to share them. Share and share again, with a generous heart so others may be inspired and know. So I may use you in this way, go and share! I will never leave you but always greatly anticipate you! I will be thinking about the enjoyment that we will have again, in these kinds of ways in the near future. We will be awaiting your next arrival, while always looking into you with love."

After Jesus said this, I was back where I started these journeys, but I was not the same. I was shocked, honored, amazed, felt so loved, and was extremely determined! I noticed that I was filling my journal. I had filled the pages above while being in heavenly places, and with the Holy Spirit. I was aware that I was encountering God through our shared writing, but beginning to understand it was still so astounding! The Holy Spirit led and guided me to do what would seem impossible! I had written about my experiences in these places, while having them at the same time, in raw expression and vulnerability! Heavenly destination after heavenly destination, I got to experience the love of the Holy Trinity and spend in-depth time with the *original Father* and the *original Son*.

I was changed, challenged, healed, upgraded, and brought into God's promises! He shared so much of His beauty and His broad grandeur with me. In an instant, my mindset and my whole life were transformed. Every part of the core of who I am shines brighter now. I now know how to react in vibrant, ordained movement more fluently when God boldly, gently, and carefully works on my clay structure. I am no longer a still porcelain doll. I am a daughter of Father God, who knows how to carry my birthright with Him! I surely do have far more than a book to share. From destination to destination, the journeys have just begun.

INVITATIONS FOR JESUS AND THE HOLY SPIRIT

I wanted to write an invitation for anyone who becomes inspired to welcome Jesus and know Him, as well as the Holy Spirit, through this book. If you want to know Jesus, then I encourage you to take the words below and turn them into your prayer. Whether you want to know Him for the first time or want to renew your dedication.

"Jesus, I believe You are the Son of God. I believe that You died on the cross for all my sins and, because of that, I am forgiven. I repent of all my sins and ask You to forgive me. I ask You to come into my heart and to have an everlasting relationship with You. In the name of Jesus Christ. Amen."

> *For God so [greatly] loved and dearly prized the world, that He [even] gave His [One and] only begotten Son, so that whoever believes and trusts in Him [as Savior] shall not perish but have eternal life.* (John 3:16 AMP)

I also wanted to include an invitation to the Holy Spirit. If this book has inspired you in any way to have a relationship with the Holy Spirit and experience what seems impossible, then I encourage you to invite Him to fill your life, after accepting Jesus. Again, you can use the words below and turn them into your prayer.

"Holy Spirit, I want to know You and more about myself through You. I ask You to baptize and fill me as You come into the room and my life. To bring me to places I have only dreamed of and to bring me into the complete fullness God has for my life. Please do this, so I may know all of who God is. I pray this in Jesus's name. Amen."

KEY SCRIPTURES THAT BRING THIS BOOK LIFE

But he said, Yea rather, blessed are they that hear the word of God, and keep it. (Luke 11:28 ASV)

My flesh and my heart faileth; But God is the strength of my heart and my portion forever. (Psalm 73:26 ASV)

Let the word of Christ live in you richly, flooding you with all wisdom. Apply the Scriptures as you teach and instruct one another with the Psalms, and with festive praises, and with prophetic songs given to you spontaneously by the Spirit, so sing to God with all your hearts! Let every activity of your lives and every word that comes from your lips be drenched with the beauty of our Lord Jesus, the Anointed One. And bring your constant praise to God the Father because of what Christ has done for you! (Colossians 3:16–17 TPT)

Whoever exalts himself shall be humbled; and whoever humbles himself shall be raised to honor. (Mathew 23:12 AMP)

When you pass through the waters, I will be with you; And through the rivers, they will not overwhelm you. When you walk through fire, you will not be scorched, Nor will the flame burn you. (Isaiah 43:2 AMP)

Have I not commanded you? Be strong and courageous! Do not be terrified or dismayed (intimidated), for the Lord your God is with you wherever you go. (Joshua 1:9 AMP)

Cast your burden on the LORD [release it] and He will sustain and uphold you; He will never allow the righteous to be shaken (slip, fall, fail). (Psalm 55:22 AMP)

And be not fashioned according to this world: but be ye transformed by the renewing of your mind, that ye may prove what is the good and acceptable and perfect will of God. (Romans 12:2 ASV)

Jesus said to him, "What do you mean 'if'? If you are able to believe, all things are possible to the believer." (Mark 9:23 TPT)

I know what it means to lack, and I know what it means to experience overwhelming abundance. For I'm trained in the secret of overcoming all things, whether in fullness or in hunger. And I find that the strength of Christ's explosive power infuses me to conquer every difficulty. (Philippians 4:12–13 TPT)

THINGS WHICH THE EYE HAS NOT SEEN AND THE EAR HAS NOT HEARD, AND WHICH HAVE NOT ENTERED THE HEART OF MAN, ALL THAT GOD HAS PREPARED FOR THOSE WHO LOVE HIM [who hold Him in affectionate reverence, who obey Him, and who grate-

fully recognize the benefits that He has bestowed]. (1 Corinthians 2:9 AMP)

In the beginning [before all time] was the Word (Christ), and the Word was with God, and the Word was God Himself. (John 1:1 AMP)

Oh that my words were now written! Oh that they were inscribed in a book! That with an iron pen and lead
They were graven in the rock for ever! (Job 19:23–24 ASV)

Then I said, "Behold, I come [to the throne];
In the scroll of the book it is written of me. (Psalm 40:7 AMP)

You have taken account of my wanderings;
Put my tears in Your bottle.
Are they not recorded in Your book? (Psalm 56:8 AMP)

And I will ask the Father and he will give you another Savior, the Holy Spirit of Truth, who will be to you a friend just like me—and he will never leave you. The world won't receive him because they can't see him or know him. But you know him intimately because he remains with you and will live inside you. (John 14:16–17 TPT)

You formed my innermost being, shaping my delicate inside and my intricate outside, and wove them all together in my mother's womb.
I thank you, God, for making me so mysteriously complex! Everything you do is marvelously

breathtaking. It simply amazes me to think about it! How thoroughly you know me, Lord!

You even formed every bone in my body when you created me in the secret place; carefully, skillfully you shaped me from nothing to something. You saw who you created me to be before I became me! Before I'd ever seen the light of day, the number of days you planned for me were already recorded in your book. Every single moment you are thinking of me! How precious and wonderful to consider that you cherish me constantly in your every thought! O God, your desires toward me are more than the grains of sand on every shore! When I awake each morning, you're still with me. (Psalm 139:13–18 TPT)

For this is the hope of our salvation. But hope means that we must trust and wait for what is still unseen. For why would we need to hope for something we already have? So because our hope is set on what is yet to be seen, we patiently keep on waiting for its fulfillment. And in a similar way, the Holy Spirit takes hold of us in our human frailty to empower us in our weakness. For example, at times we don't even know how to pray, or know the best things to ask for. But the Holy Spirit rises up within us to super-intercede on our behalf, pleading to God with emotional sighs too deep for words. (Romans 8:24–26 TPT)

But whenever you pray, go into your innermost chamber and be alone with Father God, praying to him in secret. And your Father, who sees all you do, will reward you openly. (Matthew 6:6 TPT)

When the Israelites saw it, they said to one another, "What is it?" For they did not know what it was. And Moses said to them, "This is the bread which the Lord has given you to eat. (Exodus 16:15 KJV)

He that hath an ear, let him hear what the Spirit saith unto the churches; To him that overcometh will I give to eat of the hidden manna, and will give him a white stone, and in the stone a new name written, which no man knoweth saving he that receiveth it. (Revelation 2:17 KJV)

And Peter answered him and said, Lord, if it be thou, bid me come unto thee on the water. And he said, Come. And when Peter was come down out of the ship, he walked on the water, to go to Jesus. (Matthew 14:28–29 KJV)

But without faith it is impossible to please him: for he that cometh to God must believe that he is, and that he is a rewarder of them that diligently seek him. (Hebrews 11:6 KJV)

INTRIGUING SYMBOLISMS

Page 17: The discoloration that left my legs—weakness, and what felt like imperfection, to me.

Pages 16 and 17: The defining and refining of my muscles and appearance—strength and transformation.

Pages 18 and 19: Misty Manna—the yellow heavenly presence mist can have one wondering, *What is it?*

Pages 11 and 12: Pearl—the pearl is the birthstone for the month that I was born in; I was born in June.

Page 11: Candy—sweet and hidden delight that God had saved for just the right time.

Pages 10, 16, and 19: Clothing—The putting on of something new.

Page 20: Blankets—The coverings of a new day and a new night. New action during the day with the Holy Spirit and new intimacy during the night with the Holy Spirit.

ABOUT THE AUTHOR

Haley Keen is a born and raised West Texan who loves to write, paint, act, and drink coffee. She has been writing since the age of fourteen and has also been involved in local acting since she was a child. She attends church regularly, as well as Bible school. She believes in the power of the Word of God and in having a relationship with Him. It is in her heart to influence her generation through her writing, as she is a young writer. It is her hope that her books bring encouragement to people and let them know how much God loves them.